DRAFT VICINITY
by
SCOTT THURSTON

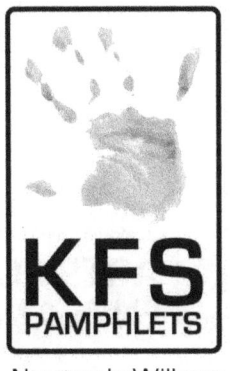

Newton-le-Willows

Published in the United Kingdom in 2018
by The Knives Forks And Spoons Press,
51 Pipit Avenue,
Newton-le-Willows,
Merseyside,
WA12 9RG.

ISBN 978-1-912211-16-6

Copyright © Scott Thurston, 2018.

The right of Scott Thurston to be identified as the author of this work has been asserted by them in accordance with the Copyrights, Designs and Patents Act of 1988. All rights reserved. No part of this publication may be reproduced, stored in a retrieval system, transmitted in any form or by any means, electronic, photocopying, recording or otherwise, without prior permission of the publisher.

A Note on the Cover

Cover image by Scott Thurston from sketches in biro made during *Drawn Together Drawn Apart* — a collaboration between artists and dancers curated by Joseph Lau which took place at the University of Salford's Media City UK campus in June 2014. Thanks to Camilla Luff for inviting me — you are in my drawings!

TABLE OF CONTENTS

Poem	7
What is the Language Using Us For?	8
Sanctified	9
The Colours of the State	10
Café Bleu	13
Colloquium	14
The Ship Overwhelmed by Nature	15
This is Privilege	16
Movement Study I	17
Movement Study II	18
Cloth Cat	19
When the River Throws	20
Winter Garden	22
You Thought it Didn't Need Saying	23
Bury Market	24
Improvisations	25
Diamond. Volcano. Myrrh.	27
Vitality Dynamics	28
A635	29
Untitled	30
Acknowledgments	32

DRAFT VICINITY

POEM

In your situation suddenly into
a process you cannot deplete.
What was enlarged before,
fell back into a strait – the
everyday of the subtle's bloom
turns to breached oxygen.

You wonder to modelled account
interminable translation resources
apprehension pattern contracts
into workable confines a huge cut
satisfaction in deficit – breach the lip.

Scott Thurston

WHAT IS THE LANGUAGE USING US FOR?
after a line by W. S. Graham

Yes, this is it. You can't make it go
Further than this, building out of
The pattern of thought.

You can only go on from where it is,
Not leaping over but encountering
Whatever is to hand.

To be clear about a certain limited
Grounding, an anachronistic gesture.
To define select terms to a

Common committee: an intention to
Balance the weight of experience.
Drafting out a panel

Of exclamations to acknowledge that
Life *is*, that it turns us about in itself.
Determine generative accounts

Full into the indexed balance of war.
Wanting to root into the particulars –
That nothing stay hidden.

SANCTIFIED

She's got a ticket to ride
brought her a spell
collapsed over the sea
to Ireland.

A terse buffeting brought
her round in the shape
of erotic space to
be worthy of it.

Bamboozled by currency
value of things undreamt
of lines in close
circumspect familiarity.

Kavanagh's agonising
pincer jaws I could
not dare to dream
heaven-sent.

Poet, baffled by the
trade in conversation,
try to accept *not*
knowing – harsh
unglamorous light of
this art.

Scott Thurston

THE COLOURS OF THE STATE
for and after Rachel Warriner's *Red / Blue / Yellow*

step to the side
unfold the abstract
index sudden solidity
tries different strategies
beyond expectation
sketches the shape of
a thought and moves
on neurological cast
open mine shallow
wake to a stunning
pacific rhythm
nonchalance by chance
cheaply born or won
to attest to tumult
synthetic project
catapult a series of
solutions onto
mezzanine bar what
sound attempts
bridge gaps in
turned knowledge
process to tamp
down load in
mysterious circs
don't doubt it
fallen foreign
subtleties lost
on deranged swordship
backed-up roundels

over-expressed decks
upended to siren
dance smart water
scan cable thieves
punching through
consciousness
find that relation
steady enough to
paint an emotion
passing through
a membrane
taut to string
along the neat
attempt I thought
I told you to begin
your renunciations
of slides feints and
falls into ignorance
lovely show reserves
attempt conserves
contempt left to
describe a longer
turn around term
to trace progress
installing a model
regretful derivation
hide-bound extraction
supportive inklings
broken braced against
a stupid blunt axle
your deluded sacrifice
attributed noble
pose to justify base

inequality and terminal
terrace bottomed up
to top in tight
trauma of your free
association simple
words timed to expand
waste expenditure
drawn out over
the troubled surface
capital invests with
mystique what chance
you slipped through
a gap in that other
life of yours
hours to time a
skilled landscape
assault punched
through the face
whilst the state
continues its
ministry of misery
too cold the tone
of the whole
in false recompense
offered to burn itself
off in refined
conditions

CAFÉ BLEU

What is my science? On this
Cool threshold, tilting the reed
To my lips, light falls and fails,
Straggling across the skeins of clustered
Pots in the darkness. Outside, the light
Of day could make more effort
But is basically encouraging to your
Thoughts and aims, your desire for
Refreshment and music. But these
Dull pots are etched by cosmic cat's
Cradle traceries delineating the subtle
Metaphysics of soul-assisted travel –
Each to their own announcing the
Next coding – strange attractors to draw
You in and out across your sax's shuddering lips.

COLLOQUIUM

you thought that the
argument could have got
out the pattern edged
through the gut punched
on both fronts wanting
reconciliation at the price
of supplication took its
toll to bespoke overtures
and retrievals troubled
inequities across a costed
bound to flip a tense
bird macho man
thought to bury thought
to contest whilst dis-
avowing ego ignominy
attention unfolded full
mediocrity in the median
mode is not a judgement
that manipulated your
ambitions the exact
opposite of what you de-
clare to tamp turned
out and over ashes of
survival in a crumb of
burned out porcelain
simple sonnet something
beyond the pale could
not advance your artificial
objectives to have your
art and eat it out

THE SHIP OVERWHELMED BY NATURE

    extensive colour
      serve to defy nature, her distress alert may go unheard
Seeing
that nature prior to the Dead
of overwhelming ship in
Canada formally 'Slave
Ship' forward,
    charting
forces or was outside
 of overboard
 the ship moving
forward,
charting,
to defy nature, her distress
may go
    unheard...seeing force...seeing
    to defy
nature.

Due to perish even
    more of my
    business at the viewer feel
even more overwhelmed
the normal ship
 as a viable
carrier
of
the Idea
that a Pilot steams to defy nature, her
  distress at the ship as a
picture, her distress

THIS IS PRIVILEGE

of
     the constitution roadmap and its width
  every advantage,
I was brought up with ever,
  I bought
up with papers
    folded
  that I would cancel the contract at the term
  white piece of the
contract
on a clipboard
with
     installation
roadmap and
customer service, I decided back, obscuring the
    contract

at this once. Nobody
  will ever,
     every advantage

MOVEMENT STUDY I

Walking on the spot, then moving from
Side to side. Bending from the waist,
Sliding into a crouch, then stretching
Out – straightening the legs, crown first.

Flexion, balance, skin: mover moving with sound
In constructive rest. The hand placed over
The jugular notch, floating boxes under the skin,
The body part grounded, part aerial.

The vertical axis line – placing hands behind
The head and at the feet, chest and abdomen.
Taking the weight of the arms, placing hands
Under the scapulae, under the sacroiliac joint.

Taking the weight of the legs and folding them
Back into the body and applying pressure.
The underscore of potential poems, the interchange
Between body and environment.

MOVEMENT STUDY II

in the familiarity of the studio the
return of death crimps the knee
expands out to the right

not being as present the common
narrative the elbows above the
sternum lean forearms into face

left leg points, expands, extends
fertile territory where films lie
being here and to work at being here

the absence of film being a
mechanical expansion into space
with limbs, spine opening

sending heel of hand into floor
recruits spatial flesh necessarily
sit down to write on dirty floor

body folded like a scarf in tripped
time frames subtle to open up in
feeling like a threat body controlled

by weight of the pen

CLOTH CAT

In the shop of lost
objects, a broken vessel

emerges from a vessel.
We hear a song, repeated.

Then the cat in the cap
weaves a tale to put it back

together again. The vessel
restored to its vessel,

the whole placed in the
window for the one who

has lost it, one day
to collect it.

Scott Thurston

WHEN THE RIVER THROWS

when the river throws
a green light
you excel in

when the river
throws
a green light

when the port buoys
on the river
flash green

in succession

you excel in surveying
the possibilities from the
little hill

when the starboard buoys throw
out red light

you think of the green
you excel in flash

you look on from the hill
fifteen years ago

this river these buoys
these lights studding
the banks in the twilight

the river throws these
green, red lights
you excel in

WINTER GARDEN
for Gwyn Jones

something has contracted
yet some turgid sap
still humble enough
circulates through bamboo,
vines and poison ivy
your evergreen sheen
at large
by light
mirror displacements, classical
fragments and york stone
flags sunken by the
fountain bleak fertility
of ideas
come to light

YOU THOUGHT IT DIDN'T NEED SAYING

The ideal and real meet in me
like a tool and die. Children as intent
circle in the park: would this street
cloy, would these strata separate and

refold? I am always working when I am
not working, when I am not working
I am working. The real reels from
this ideal.

      To deal in the real big deal,
Not ideal. I prefer the term, to give
A house a home in this daily history.

To release the word of the constraint
of its thought:
           float or hem a rare hew.

BURY MARKET

still working at the market
stall resisting that mental
shot to fall in love yet again
a thousand casual encounters

in these aisles female and male
relations pursued by black dogs
in personalised collars the shoes
piled-up like the museum cabinet

these things that live through us
turn into our turn on
trash at the book clearance

that no-one covets the stall
I must still work at it
live in its draft vicinity

IMPROVISATIONS

When you went to the draining board you noticed the thin strip of water still clinging to the blade of the vegetable knife, so you decided to wipe it on a tea towel before you sliced the banana into the muesli, the tuberous shape falling away in thick discs. The space you co-inhabit beckons the shape of a running cat sketched on a note attached to the foil that contains a sandwich made for your lunch at work: traced observations of the world we share.

*

Reading a fragment of 'Little Gidding' reminds you of walking in winter woods near a field which you used to visit to camp on Scout exercises. It was called Birchmere. In the wood were long straight ditches cut for drainage, and on this occasion, they had frozen so solidly and completely, one could see right through the surface down to a bed of dead leaves on the bottom. In our hiking boots we thrilled to run up and see how far we could slide down the ice.

*

Whence this energy? This is not for you. The comfort of the safe neighbourhood, with effective boundaries. The comfort of a decent stock of knowledge, well-maintained, the ease of the tenure.

*

Conducting your relationship to yourself with tenderness. That you are here, now, and can only go on from that point, sun reflecting off the brickwork, the cement. Searching for the sources of industry, break open that space-time.

*

Taking the drawers outside to clean them in the sunny yard. Washing them off with the detergent, then rinsing them in hot water, drying them off with a tea-towel. Cleaning out the castors from a foul mixture of dried food and hair.

*

That if what you think with is both Clark Coolidge and Mei-mei Berssenbrugge – trying to find permissions in the interstices for your humble, creaky, leaky craft.

*

Foot solid grows what soil this

*

the concern about the lights
about to go out wasted resources
wasted energy it cannot serve
me here where I stand where
I have to make the centre fit
for consumption of an elastic kind
of thinking not hide into a binding
hard of hearing

*

Yes, a sense it's still possible to be walking home down the street, wearing jeans, with a bag over your shoulder about quarter to eight in the evening. That the movement has purpose, meaning, is complete and precise whatever else it might contain about the trials and tribulations of the day.

DIAMOND. VOLCANO. MYRRH.
for Billie Hanne

You saw how you thought you wanted it,
how my space sounded out your move
into and out of you. There is no time or space
for all this to fit into anymore, only the set tight
longing tight in the heart for all your open purchases.

You thought my life determined me out
of those perspectives, but it turned in on itself,
slipping along those surfaces. It's not a bad
movie, but the reel sticks beckoning
a flat charge of packed glycerol, bursting

at the seams. What knowledge brings was
always a double-edged cake walk on a knife
to scrape the gut back into relevance.
Forgot to bring you back to me, hurt suddenly
for a song to subtle traces shimmering

through the night air for a concrete platform.
Expendable, troubled, over-determined, your
largesse beckons the bow-wave forward full-
throttle to slide that launch home again. Dipping
through wavelengths a self dispersed,

recollected on a silver platter, backed
to dump all forward craft out of the ocean.
Damaged in the heat, intent inscribes
muscular intelligence brought back,
suddenly overstanding its self-harm.

VITALITY DYNAMICS
for Lou Rowan and Andrea Augé

that we enter into movement
as if against a sky borne
in it, are in it, have it in
us to consequence this into
shape sets spins out of it
to turn touch away from
opened source breaks down
our indivisional requisites
for which we span a tidal
distal wave to number
dynamic manifold envelope
in space-time, force, direction
as intended gestural outcome

let's span a wasted flare
gain backdrop uplift
to scissor through sound

A635

carve something
out of business
mist over road
covers over
measure to re-
assure a particle
where you took
refuge
        reassure
that measure of a
tibial stretch agenda
began again as
mist crusts the
road crushes the
abode abiding in
your business

UNTITLED

there are some platforms
that you have not sought yet
where that authority becomes
your majority – not quite
written out of town
                      your gap on a
chair dares to stare all
this bleakness down to
an assumed identity
traced across – a blacklist
                      to pare all
this whiteness out tamps
that material break this
effortless night all right

ACKNOWLEDGMENTS

I wish to gratefully acknowledge the editors of these publications in which some of these poems first appeared:

Alan Corkish and Andy Taylor for 'Poem' 'What is the Language Using Us for?' and 'Sanctified' in *Erbacce* 28 (2012)

Robert Kiely for 'The Colours of the State' in *Orra* 5: the Technology Issue (2013)

Martin Stannard for 'Colloquium' in *August 1, 2013* (augustone2013.blogspot.co.uk)

Jack Boulton for 'This is Privilege' in *Hand Picked Stimulus Respond* (2014)

James Byrne for 'You Thought It Didn't Need Saying' in *The Wolf* (2014)

Special thanks to Gareth Farmer for initiating a poetic exchange which led to the composition of 'The Ship Overwhelmed by Nature.'

Special thanks to Sarie Mairs Slee for our collaborative work with dance and poetry that led to 'Movement Study I' and 'Movement Study II,' and so much more.

Special thanks to Billie Hanne for her extraordinary poetry and dance performance workshop 'Diamond. Volcano. Myrrh.' which took place at Goldsmiths, University of London in July 2015. All the material in the poem was generated in the workshop.

Special thanks to Alec Newman for this book and the appearance of 'Bury Market' as a light-box in the 2017 Blackpool Illuminations.

www.ingramcontent.com/pod-product-compliance
Lightning Source LLC
Chambersburg PA
CBHW031509040426
42444CB00007B/1265